Sandy Creek
NEW YORK

An Imprint of Sterling Publishing
387 Park Avenue South
New York, NY 10016

This 2013 edition published by Sandy Creek.

Series creator: David Salariya
Author: Carolyn Franklin
Editor: Jamie Pitman
Illustrations: David Antram

ISBN 978-1-4351-5035-5 (HB)

Manufactured in Heshan, Guangdong Province, China
Lot #:
2 4 6 8 10 9 7 5 3 1
06/13

Top 10 Worst™ Scary Dinosaurs you wouldn't want to meet!

Raaaaar!

Created & designed by
David Salariya

Illustrated by
David Antram

Sandy Creek
NEW YORK

Written by
Carolyn Franklin

Contents

The Age of dinosaurs 5

All shapes and sizes! 6

Were all dinosaurs scary? 8

No. 10: Masiakasaurus 10

No. 9: Eocarcharia dinops 12

No. 8: Triceratops 14

No. 7: Quetzalcoatlus 16

No. 6: Troodon 18

No. 5: Kronosaurus 20

No. 4: Allosaurus 22

No. 3: Megaraptor 24

No. 2: Tyrannosaurus rex 26

No. 1: Spinosaurus 28

Glossary 30

Index 32

The Age of dinosaurs

For over 160 million years during the Mesozoic Era, dinosaurs were the dominant creatures on Earth. These incredible creatures became extinct 65 mya (million years ago). Dinosaurs were prehistoric reptiles, and most of them hatched from eggs. The ten scary dinosaurs in this book were all fearsome killers, but for ten very different reasons.

In the beginning!

All the animals below are related to each other. Dinosaurs, such as those on this page, evolved from a group of primitive reptiles, which were related to present-day crocodiles. *Deinonychus* belonged to a group of amazing dinosaurs that could be the ancestors of modern birds.

Pteranodon *was a flying reptile, but not a dinosaur!*
Wingspan: 25 ft (7.6 m)
Lived: 85–65 mya

Diplodocus
Length: 85 ft (26 m)
Lived: 155–145 mya

Modern pigeon
Wingspan: 12 in (30 cm)

Deinonychus
Length: 10 ft (3 m)
Lived: 120–110 mya

Modern crocodile
Length: 10–15 ft (3–4.6 m)

Stegosaurus
Length: 20–25 ft (6–7.6 m)
Lived: 150–140 mya

All shapes and sizes!

There were many different types of dinosaurs. Some lived in extremely hot and cold habitats, and had to adapt to the environment in order to survive. Varying greatly in size, some were the largest animals to ever walk on Earth, whereas others were no bigger than a chicken. While many dinosaurs were able to run fast, others were slow and lumbering. Some walked on two legs, others on four, and some dinosaurs could even do both.

Iguanodon *walked on all fours but probably stood on its hind legs to feed on taller plants.*

Gigantic, slow-moving dinosaurs like Brachiosaurus *had pillar-like legs to support their tremendous weight.*

Albertosaurus could run as fast as 28 miles (45 km) per hour on its two strong back legs.

Brachiosaurus

6   Iguanodon

Albertosaurus

Mesozoic era

No one type of dinosaur lasted for the whole of the Mesozoic Era. They evolved during the Triassic Period (c.250–213 mya), and lived through the Jurassic and Cretaceous Periods (c.213–c. 65 mya). Then, towards the end of the Cretaceous Period, they became extinct. Dinosaurs were constantly evolving, and the first dinosaurs that appeared in the early Jurassic Period were mostly very different from those still alive at the end of the Cretaceous Period.

End of the Cretaceous Period (c.65 mya)

Start of the Cretaceous Period (c.144 mya)

Start of the Jurassic Period (c.213 mya)

Start of the Triassic Period. (c.250 mya)

Modern fish, flowering plants, and birds evolve.

The end of the Jurassic Period. The earliest dinosaurs evolve.

Many of the largest dinosaurs evolve.

Dinosaurs are widespread on the supercontinent.

The first dinosaurs evolve.

The time spiral of the Mesozoic era starts at the bottom, showing Earth 250 mya. It winds upward, showing the different periods when the dinosaurs evolved. It stops around 65 mya, when the dinosaurs and many other prehistoric animals died out.

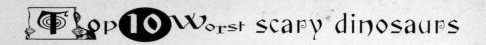

Were all dinosaurs scary?

The majority of dinosaurs were herbivores (plant eaters) and omnivores (plant and meat eaters). However, the remaining dinosaurs were bloodthirsty, flesh-eating carnivores!

fast food

Oviraptor—a small omnivorous dinosaur—had a parrot-like head; a short, toothless beak; and very powerful jaws. Its diet consisted of meat, eggs, seeds, insects, and plants. *Oviraptor* had two long, thin, bird-like legs and could run up to 43 miles (70 km) per hour, which is as fast as an ostrich living in the present day.

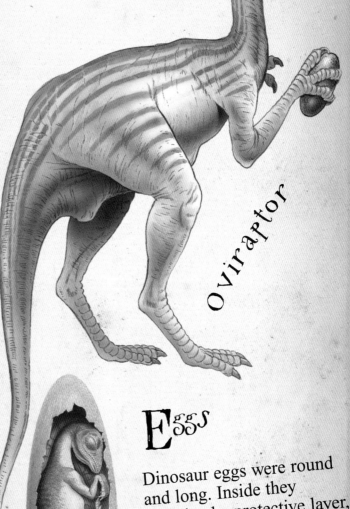

Oviraptor

found innocent

Paleontologists found a fossilized *Oviraptor* on top of some dinosaur eggs, and for many years they believed that the *Oviraptor* had been eating them. Later evidence showed that the *Oviraptor* was actually a parent of the eggs in the nest, and not an egg thief after all!

Eggs

Dinosaur eggs were round and long. Inside they contained a protective layer, called the amnion, that helped to keep the dinosaur embryo moist.

Embryo

Amnion

Clubbed to death!

Despite their peaceful diet of plants, many of the herbivores had fiendish ways of defending themselves against bloodthirsty carnivores. *Euoplocephalus* was a large herbivorous dinosaur that was covered in armor for protection. It also had rows of large spikes along its body and horns on its head. Its club-like tail was its secret weapon, and would have been a useful defense even against a hungry *Tyrannosaurus rex*.

Killing machines

Carnivorous dinosaurs were designed to kill! Most had long, strong legs so they could run fast to chase their prey. Large, powerful jaws equipped with sharp, pointed teeth, and claws for killing and tearing the flesh of their prey completed this lethal combination.

Tyrannosaurus rex

Albertosaurus

Euoplocephalus

Thwack!

9

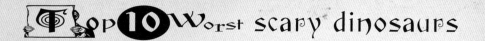

No 10

Masiakasaurus

A bipedal dinosaur with a long neck and tail, *Masiakasaurus* had one extraordinary feature—its terrifying teeth. Its long, sharp front teeth pointed forward, which is rare for predatory dinosaurs. Its vicious lower front teeth were almost horizontal, and would have been ideal for spearing prey. Its blade-like back teeth cut and ripped its victim's flesh into tasty, bite-sized chunks.

Vital statistics

Name: *Masiakasaurus* (muh-shee-uh-kuh-SOHR-uhs)
Meaning: vicious lizard
Length: up to 6 ft (2 m)
Weight: 77 lbs (35 kg)
Diet: carnivorous
Time span: about 70 mya
Period: Late Cretaceous
Found: Madagascar

You wouldn't want to know this:

A piece of fossilized dinosaur dung is called a coprolite. It can tell us how, who, and what the dinosaur ate!

Tremble!

Masiakasaurus' diet consisted of fish, lizards, and other smaller dinosaurs.

Dinosaur teeth

Scientists studying a dinosaur's fossilized teeth can discover what it ate, how it got the food, and whether it chewed, crushed, or just swallowed it whole! Teeth are harder than bone and fossilize more easily. This is how we know that some dinosaurs existed even though only their teeth remain.

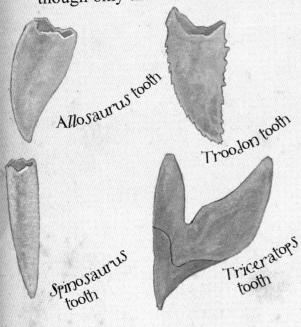

Allosaurus tooth

Troodon tooth

Spinosaurus tooth

Triceratops tooth

Gnashers!

Gallimimus

You should see how much I save on dentist's bills!

With up to 960 teeth, the herbivorous, duck-billed dinosaurs—such as *Parasaurolophus*—had more teeth than any other dinosaur. By contrast, bird-like, omnivorous dinosaurs such as *Gallimimus* and *Ornithomimus* had no teeth at all.

Parasaurolophus

Fierce carnivores like *Allosaurus* and *Tyrannosaurus rex* had sharp, pointed teeth for tearing flesh. If the dinosaur had powerful jaws, their teeth would be used for crushing their victim's bones. *Triceratops* used its toothless beak to gather up vegetation and its flat cheek teeth to chew tough plant material. *Troodon* snarled through serrated teeth, ideal for cutting through tough meat and sinews.

Mashed to a pulp

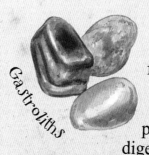

Gastroliths

The large herbivores had spoon-shaped or peg-like teeth designed for stripping plants. They didn't chew their food. Instead, the tough plant material was digested inside their huge guts. Many plant-eating dinosaurs swallowed gastroliths, or "stomach stones," which helped to grind up the leaves and twigs.

No 9

Eocarcharia dinops

The fierce-eyed dinosaur *Eocarcharia dinops* used its huge and immensely hard brow bone to butt rival males and attract potential mates. Its 3-inch- (7.6-cm-) long teeth were blade-shaped, ideal for disabling live dinosaurs and severing their body parts! The top predator of its day, *Eocarcharia's* chief prey was the long-necked plant eater *Nigersaurus*.

Vital statistics

Name:	*Eocarcharia dinops* (ee-oh-kahr-KAHR-ee-uh DY-nahps)
Meaning:	dawn shark
Length:	19–25 ft (6–8 m)
Weight:	up to 1.6 tons (1.5 metric tons)
Diet:	carnivorous
Time span:	112–99 mya
Period:	Cretaceous
Found:	Niger; North Africa

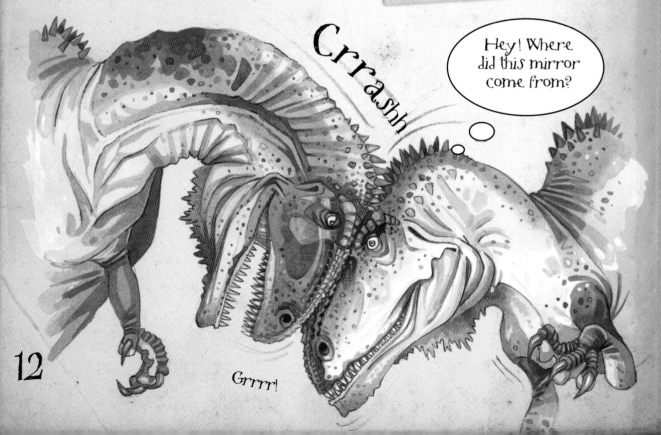

12

Granddaddy dinosaur

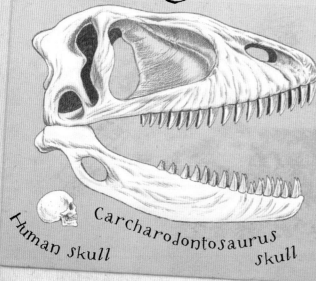

Human skull
Carcharodontosaurus skull

Over a long period of time, *Eocarcharia dinops* evolved into an even larger predator, *Carcharodontosaurus*. *Carcharodontosaurus* was a monstrous carnivore with a heavy-boned, bulky body and a massive tail. It grew up to 46 feet (15 m) long and weighed up to 15 tons (13.6 metric tons). When it reached full size, its skull was as big as a fully grown human!

Nigersaurus had a mouth shaped like the end of a vacuum cleaner. It ate vegetation from the ground like a modern cow.

Eocarcharia would have been too slow to run down most other dinosaurs. However, this deadly killer may have pounced on other dinosaurs when they weren't expecting it.

Nigersaurus

Munch!

Smack!

My mother always told me not to eat fast food!

No 8

Triceratops

Although deceptively peaceful, *Triceratops'* long horns and strong body would have made it a formidable opponent for even an aggressive carnivore like *Tyrannosaurus rex*. *Triceratops'* head alone weighed a massive 1,000 pounds (454 kg). When it charged an attack, *Triceratops'* 4-foot- (1.2-m-) long horns were capable of digging into the predator's flesh, even penetrating its heart. The solid bone attached to its skull shielded *Triceratops'* soft body from attack.

Vital statistics

Name:	*Triceratops* (try-SEHR-uh-tahps)
Meaning:	three-horned face
Length:	up to 29 ft (9 m)
Weight:	6–12 tons (5.4–10.9 metric tons)
Diet:	herbivorous
Time span:	67–65 mya
Period:	Late Cretaceous
Found:	United States

Grrrr!

Be prepared!
Always expect to read the very worst

Despite its small brain, Triceratops was one of the most successful dinosaurs of the late Cretaceous Period. It was one of the last dinosaurs to have existed.

I'm a survivor! I put it down to the fruit and veggies ... oh, and the horns!

Turning heads

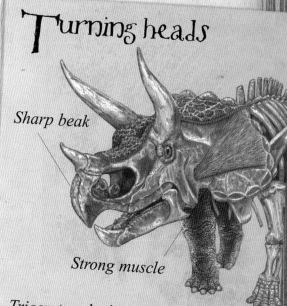

Sharp beak

Strong muscle

Triceratops had a special joint at the base of its skull, allowing it to move its head almost 360 degrees. In a fraction of a second it could position its head, ready to face a threatening predator.

Horrible horns

Triceratops probably lived in small groups. The male with the largest and sharpest horns would be capable not just of defending its territory, but also of beating a rival male when it was time to mate.

Crrunch

No 7
Quetzalcoatlus

Quetzalcoatlus was one of the largest flying creatures to ever exist. This truly terrifying creature existed during the Cretaceous period and, like the dinosaurs, was a reptile.

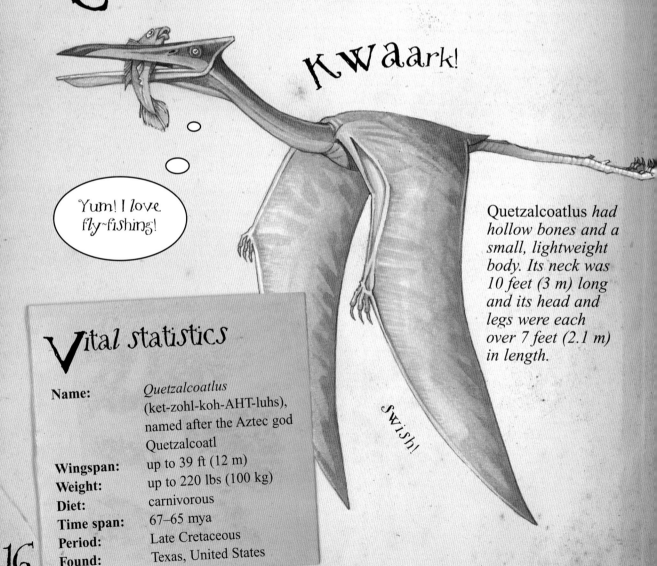

KWaark!

Yum! I love fly-fishing!

Swish!

Quetzalcoatlus *had hollow bones and a small, lightweight body. Its neck was 10 feet (3 m) long and its head and legs were each over 7 feet (2.1 m) in length.*

Vital statistics

Name: *Quetzalcoatlus* (ket-zohl-koh-AHT-luhs), named after the Aztec god Quetzalcoatl

Wingspan: up to 39 ft (12 m)

Weight: up to 220 lbs (100 kg)

Diet: carnivorous

Time span: 67–65 mya

Period: Late Cretaceous

Found: Texas, United States

Be prepared!
Always expect to read the very worst

Eagle-eyed

Whoosh!

The wings of *Quetzalcoatlus* were covered by a thin, leathery layer that stretched between its body, the top of its legs, and its long fourth fingers. Claws protruded from the other fingers. It was able to soar vast distances and it had good eyesight, which it used to spot prey from the air. A flock of these incredible animals must have been an absolutely awesome sight!

Corpse eater

Quetzalcoatlus lived inland, near freshwater lakes. It hunted fish by gliding over water and using its long, toothless jaws to scoop up and filter its prey. *Quetzalcoatlus* was also a gruesome scavenger, walking on all fours in order to feed on the bodies of dead dinosaurs.

Chomp!

What can I say? He had a lot of guts!

Although it wasn't technically a dinosaur, Quetzalcoatlus *was a distant cousin to the dinosaurs. This huge flying reptile is included in this book because it was an incredibly scary creature!*

No 6

Troodon

What made *Troodon* more frightening than other larger, carnivorous dinosaurs was its big brain and the ability to hunt at night, sometimes in packs. A group of hungry *Troodon* would be absolutely terrifying, eating just about anything they could slash and tear apart with their sharp teeth and huge, sickle-shaped toe claws.

Raaar!

Troodon

Saurornithoides

Vital statistics

Name:	*Troodon* (TROH-oh-dahn)
Meaning:	wounding tooth
Length:	up to 6.5 ft (2 m)
Weight:	110 lbs (50 kg)
Diet:	carnivorous
Time span:	74–65 mya
Period:	Late Cretaceous
Found:	United States

Be prepared!
Always expect to read the very worst

Brain box

An animal's intelligence is measured by EQ (encephalization quotient). This is the size of the brain compared to the size of the body. The more of the body that is taken up by the brain, the more intelligent the animal.

Massospondylus, an early herbivore, had a very low EQ and was one of the least intelligent dinosaurs. *Troodon*, on the other hand, had one of the largest brains compared to the size of its body, and a higher EQ than any other dinosaur.

Massospondylus

Stalk!

Remember, boys— no growling or you'll give us away!

Egg laying

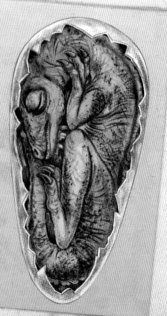

Female *Troodons* usually produced two eggs, which they incubated in earth nests. Like chickens, they often sat on the eggs, using their own body heat to warm them.

Night stalker

Troodon was only about the size of a human, so it was lightweight and able to run fast. A good sense of hearing and large, slightly forward-facing eyes allowed *Troodon* to pursue its prey in the dark.

No 5

Kronosaurus

An extremely scary marine reptile, *Kronosaurus* lived during the age of the dinosaurs. *Kronosaurus* was about the same size as a present-day sperm whale. *Kronosaurus'* sheer bulk meant it could eat almost any creature that swam past, including other marine reptiles, giant squid, large fish, and probably the occasional unlucky dinosaur that passed too close to the shore.

Vital statistics

Name:	*Kronosaurus* (kroh-noh-SOHR-uhs)
Meaning:	Kronos lizard
Length:	up to 41 ft (12.5 m)
Weight:	up to 22 tons (20 metric tons)
Diet:	carnivorous
Time span:	144–100 mya
Period:	Early Cretaceous
Found:	Australia

You wouldn't want to know this:

Kronosaurus is named after Kronos, the Greek god of time, who was so awful that he ate his own children.

Eeeeek!

And you just wanted to get your feet wet...

Sploosh!

Be prepared!
Always expect to read the very worst

Fast flippers

Kronosaurus' smooth body was driven through the water by four of the most powerful flippers ever developed by a marine animal. Capable of bursts of incredible speed, few creatures could escape it.

Big head!

This formidable predator had an enormous head, up to one third of the length of its body. Its strong jaws and 6-inch- (15-cm-) long teeth enabled it to crush the shells of giant turtles and large ammonites.

Giant squid

Car-sized turtle

Archelon was a huge turtle over 12 feet (3.6 m) long. A carnivore, *Archelon* probably ate jellyfish. When threatened by *Kronosaurus*, it would have pulled its strong flippers into its thick, protective shell.

Archelon

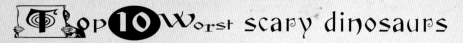

No 4

Allosaurus

The most successful carnivorous dinosaur of its time, *Allosaurus* was a fearsome, fast, and agile hunter. *Allosaurus* had a short neck, a long tail, and a massive skull with two blunt horns. Its jaws were lined with curved, dagger-like teeth, which had serrated edges like the blade of a steak knife. *Allosaurus* had strong, talon-like claws on its hands and feet, enabling it to hold down and tear at its prey, which included large herbivorous dinosaurs such as *Camptosaurus* and *Stegosaurus*.

Well, hello there!

Vital statistics

Name:	*Allosaurus* (al-uh-SOHR-uhs)
Meaning:	other lizard
Length:	up to 39 ft (12 m)
Weight:	up to 4.5 tons (4 metric tons)
Diet:	carnivorous
Time span:	153–135 mya
Period:	Late Jurassic
Found:	Tanzania; United States

Be prepared!
Always expect to read the very worst

Child care

Fossil evidence suggests that *Allosaurus* may have protected its children. It may have dragged dead carcasses back to its lair, feeding the young until they were fully grown, fending off any scavengers that might attack.

Vicious hunter

Allosaurus used its huge tail to help trap prey, and could tear the flesh off it while it was still alive! When the opportunity arose, *Allosaurus* would scavenge for food, not only eating carcasses but also driving away smaller dinosaurs from their own kills.

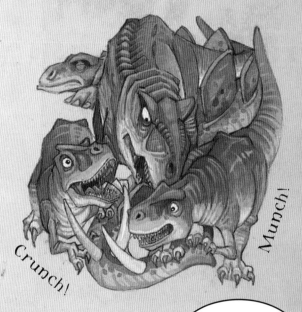

Crunch!

Munch!

Grrrr!

Growl!

Apatosaurus

Chomp!

Get off me, you big bullies!

A Little attack

Even enormous dinosaurs like *Apatosaurus* and *Diplodocus* were not safe from attack. Hunting groups of *Allosaurus* would have brought down the weakest members picked from a herd of these monster herbivores.

23

No 3

Megaraptor

The fierce, bird-like dinosaur *Megaraptor* was incredibly deadly. This extreme predator had a lethal 14-inch- (35-cm-) long, sickle-shaped claw on each foot. *Megaraptor* had a curved neck and a huge head. Its immensely powerful jaws were armed with very sharp, serrated teeth. It was an intelligent dinosaur, so if *Megaraptor* hunted in packs it could probably kill any prey it wanted.

Despite its name, Megaraptor *was not a raptor. Raptors were small to medium-sized carnivorous dinosaurs with large brains, two legs, and hands that could grasp. You can find more information about these vicious dinosaurs on the opposite page.*

Rraaaawwr!

Vital statistics

Name:	*Megaraptor* (MEH-guh-rap-tuhr)
Meaning:	huge robber
Length:	up to 26 ft (8 m)
Diet:	carnivorous
Time span:	90–84 mya
Period:	Late Cretaceous
Found:	South America

Be prepared!
Always expect to read the very worst

Terrible claw

The raptor Deinonychus *more than lived up to its name, "Terrible Claw."*

After chasing a similar-sized dinosaur like Hypsilophodon, Deinonychus overpowered its prey.

It tore open Hypsilophodon's body with its terrifying sharp-clawed fingers and sickle-like talons.

Speed kills

Zoom!

Utahraptor was one of the largest raptors that ever lived. Reaching speeds up to 62 miles (100 km) per hour, these large-eyed raptors could spot and run down any prey they chose. As pack hunters, *Utahraptors* may have used one member as bait while the others caught and killed prey up to twice their size.

Tenontosaurus

Yum! Now this is what I call fresh meat!

Chew!

Deinonychus

Working together, a group of Deinonychus, 10-foot- (3-m-) long raptors, could bring down a massive 21-foot- (6.5-m-) long Tenontosaurus.

Snarl!

25

No 2

Tyrannosaurus rex

Tyrannosaurus rex certainly was a fearsome dinosaur. This awesome carnivore had an enormous skull with massive 4-foot- (1.2-m-) long, muscular jaws packed with large, pointed teeth. It could run as fast as 15 miles (24 km) per hour.

Tyrannosaurus rex *had between 50 and 60 cone-shaped, saw-edged teeth for tearing flesh and crushing bones. They varied in size, but the largest teeth were huge, up to 13 inches (33 cm) long including the root. Like most dinosaurs, Tyrannosaurus rex's teeth were replaceable. As teeth were lost or broken from fighting or eating, new teeth grew to replace them.*

Vital statistics

Name: *Tyrannosaurus rex* (ty-raa-nuh-SOHR-uhs REHKS)
Meaning: tyrant lizard king
Length: up to 42 ft (13 m)
Weight: up to 7 tons (6.4 metric tons)
Diet: carnivorous
Time span: 68–65 mya
Period: Late Cretaceous
Found: United States; Canada; East Asia

Roar!

You wouldn't want to know this:

Tyrannosarus rex had an enormous mouth that could rip apart a carcass with frightening ease. It could eat up to 500 pounds (230 kg) of meat and bones in one bite!

That's right— "tyrant lizard KING!" Don't forget it!

Be prepared!
Always expect to read the very worst

Getting going

(a)

Tyrannosaurus *probably rested on its stomach. However, because of its weight, getting up would have been a problem.*

(b)

Tyrannosaurus *may have used its small front legs for balance as it started to rise.*

(c)

When its back legs were nearly straight, it could throw its head back, using the momentum to lift itself off the ground.

(d)

Once fully upright, Tyrannosaurus *would be ready to set out in search of food.*

Albertosaurus

Tyrannosaurus rex

Crunch!

Daspletosarus

Chomp!

Munch!

What a smell!

Although *Tyrannosaurus rex* hunted alone, a heightened sense of smell helped it find dead flesh when there was little live meat around. *Tyrannosaurus* dismembered and ate the dead animal quickly: the stench of a rotting carcass would have attracted scavengers from far off. *Albertosaurus* and *Daspletosaurus*, which were both relatives of *Tyrannosaurus*, would have joined in the feast.

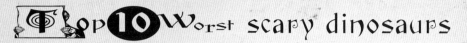

No 1

Spinosaurus

The largest carnivorous dinosaur that we know of was the very scary *Spinosaurus*, which could grow to an amazing 59 feet (18 m) long! This merciless dinosaur would attack and eat smaller prey of any kind, as well as scavenging from dead dinosaurs. Like a present-day crocodile, its long, narrow snout contained jaws filled with short, sharp, straight teeth, and its nostrils faced upwards. This meant that it was probably able to hunt sharks and other fish in nearby mangrove swamps.

Eeek!

Vital statistics

Name:	*Spinosaurus* (spy-nuh-SOHR-uhs)
Meaning:	spiny lizard
Length:	up to 59 ft (18 m)
Weight:	4–8 tons (3.6–7.2 metric tons)
Diet:	carnivorous
Time span:	about 95 mya
Period:	Late Cretaceous
Found:	Egypt; Morocco

Dimetrodon

Dimetrodon, a fierce carnivore, lived nearly 200 million years before *Spinosaurus*. It also had a sail along its back. *Dimetrodon* was an early reptile, an ancestor to the mammals, called a pelycosaur.

Hot or cold?

The distinctive spines of *Spinosaurus* grew up to 6.5 ft (2 m) long, with skin stretching between them like a sail. This sail made *Spinosaurus* appear larger and even more threatening to any rivals. Many scientists think that *Spinosaurus* also used its sail to manage its body temperature, a bit like a radiator.

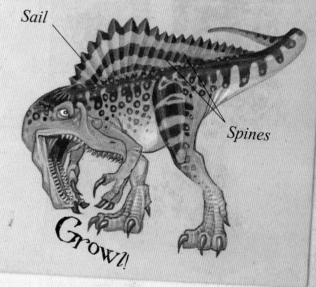

Sail

Spines

Growl!

Little and large

Spinosaurus probably had the longest head of any known carnivorous dinosaur! Its mouth was nearly 6 feet (1.8 m) long. At the other end of the scale we have the *Microraptor*, which is the tiniest dinosaur ever discovered. At only 2 feet (61 cm) long, this bizarre dinosaur had two pairs of primitive wings—one set on its forearms and the other on its hind legs. The swift-moving *Microraptor* lived in trees and fed on insects.

I'd better buzz off!

Microraptor

Raaar!

29

Glossary

Ammonite A prehistoric, fast-moving marine animal, closely related to the modern-day squid and octopus.

Amnion The thin membrane sac around a growing embryo.

Ancestor From whom a living animal is descended from.

Bipedal Standing on two feet.

Carcass The body of a dead animal.

Carnivore A meat eater.

Coprolites Preserved dung.

Diet What an animal eats.

Digested Food that has been broken down by the body.

Embryo An animal developing inside an egg.

Evolve To develop into a different form.

Extinct No longer existing or living.

Fossilized Preserved in rock or as a rock.

Gastrolith A stone swallowed by dinosaurs to enable them to digest food in their stomachs by mashing the food up.

Habitat A plant or animal's natural environment.

Herbivore A plant eater.

Incubated Kept at a particular temperature.

Lethal Deadly.

Mangrove A tropical tree growing beside water, having roots that begin aboveground.

Mammal An animal that gives birth to live young and feeds them milk from its body.

Marine Living in the sea.

Mesozoic Era A period of time which started about 250 million years ago and ended about 65 million years ago.

Omnivore Eating a variety of food including meat and plants.

Overpower To overcome by being stronger.

Paleontologist A person who studies prehistoric life.

Pelycosaur A type of prehistoric animal.

Predator An animal that kills and eats other animals.

Prehistoric The period long ago before written records were made.

Prey An animal hunted by a predator.

Primitive An early stage of evolution.

Reptile A cold-blooded vertebrate that breathes air and has skin covered with scales.

Scavenger An animal that searches for decaying flesh for food.

Serrated Saw-like. Having a row of sharp or tooth-like projections.

Sickle A type of curved knife.

Sinew A tough band of tissue that usually connects muscle to bone.

Supercontinent In prehistoric times, a single, immense mass of land consisting of all the modern continents before they broke apart.

Talon A sharp claw.

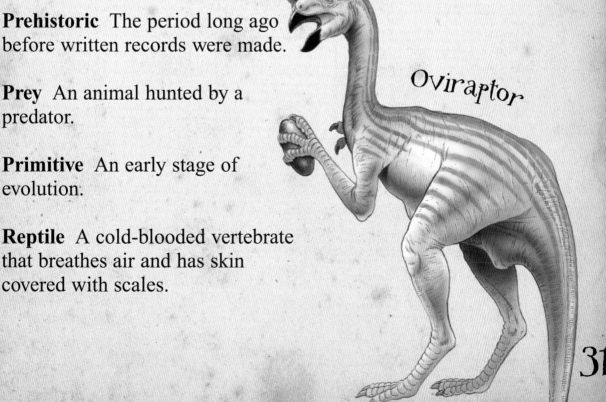

Oviraptor

Top 10 Worst scary dinosaurs

Index

A
Albertosaurus 6, 9, 27
Allosaurus 11, 22, 23
ammonites 21
amnion 8
Apatosaurus 23
Archelon 21
armor 9

B
birds 5, 7
Brachiosaurus 6

C
Camptosaurus 22
Carcharodontosaurus 13
carnivores 8–14, 16, 18,
   20–22, 24, 26, 28, 29
coprolites 10
Cretaceous Period 7, 10, 12,
   14–16, 18, 20, 24, 26, 28
crocodiles 5, 28

D
Daspletosaurus 27
defense 9, 15
Deinonychus 5, 25
Dimetrodon 29
Diplodocus 5, 23

E
eggs 5, 8, 19
embryo 8
Eocarcharia dinops 12, 13
Euoplocephalus 9
extinction 5, 7

F
fossils 8, 10, 11, 23

G
Gallimimus 11
gastroliths 11
giant squid 20, 21

H
habitats 6
herbivores 8, 9, 11, 14, 19,
   22, 23
Hypsilophodon 25

I
Iguanodon 6
intelligence 15, 18, 19, 24

J
Jurassic Period 7, 22

K
Kronosaurus 20, 21

M
Masiakasaurus 10
Massospondylus 19
Megaraptor 24
Mesozoic Era 5, 7
Microraptor 29

N
Nigersaurus 12, 13

O
omnivores 8, 11
Ornithomimus 11
Oviraptor 8

P
Parasaurolophus 11
pelycosaurs 29
predators 10, 12–15, 21, 24
prey 9, 10, 12, 17, 19,
   22–25, 28
Pteranodon 5

Q
Quetzalcoatlus 16, 17

R
raptors 24, 25
reptiles 5, 16, 17, 20, 29

S
Saurornithoides 18
scavengers 17, 23, 27, 28
Spinosaurus 11, 28, 29
Stegosaurus 5, 22

T
teeth 8–12, 18, 21, 22, 24,
   26, 28
Tenontosaurus 25
Triassic Period 7
Triceratops 11, 14, 15
Troodon 11, 18, 19
Tyrannosaurus rex 9, 11, 14,
   26, 27

U
Utahraptor 25

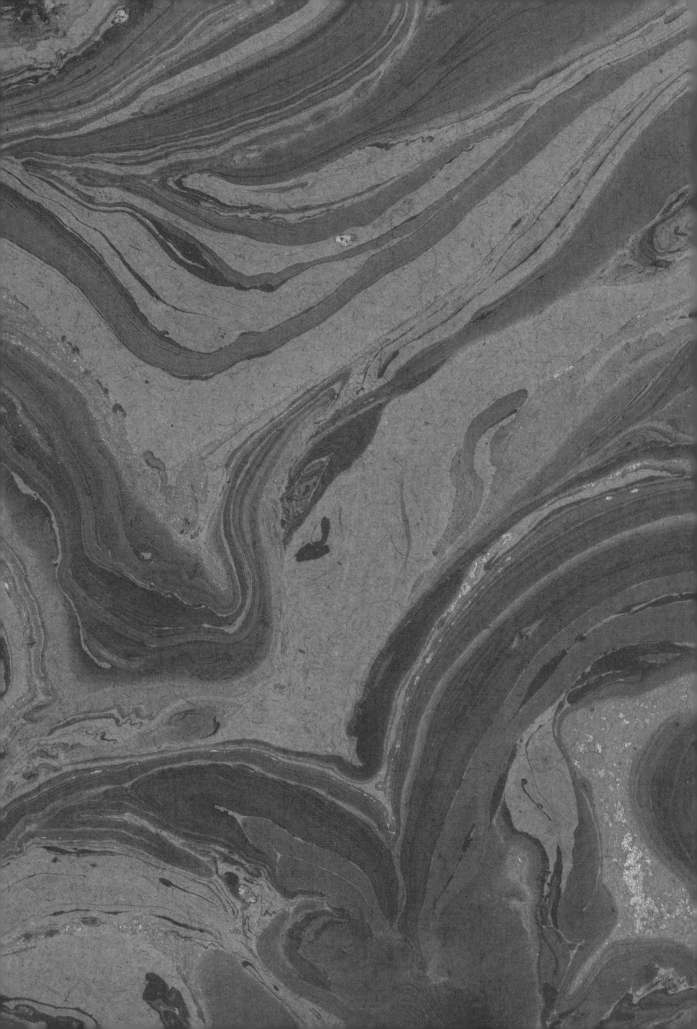